HIDDEN TREASURE

ALISON HAWES

Badger Publishing Limited
Oldmedow Road,
Hardwick Industrial Estate,
King's Lynn PE30 4JJ
Telephone: 01438 791037

www.badgerlearning.co.uk

2 4 6 8 10 9 7 5 3

Hidden Treasure ISBN 978-1-78147-553-9

Publisher: Susan Ross
Senior Editor: Danny Pearson
Designer: Fiona Grant

Photos: Cover image: REX
Page 4: Greg Balfour Evans/Alamy
Page 5: Kirsty Wigglesworth/AP/Press Association Images
Page 6: Tom Pilston/The Independent/REX
Page 7: Tom Pilston/The Independent/REX
Page 8: Kerrick James/Alamy
Page 9: Dennis Hallinan/Alamy
Page 10: Sipa Press/REX
Page 11: Nils Jorgensen/REX
Page 12: Andrey Nekrasov/Alamy
Page 13: Dr. E. Lee Spence
Page 14: De Agostini/Getty Images
Page 15: BENGT AF GEIJERSTAM/Bildhuset/TT/Press Association Images
Page 16: Katharine Andriotis Photography, LLC/Editorial/Alamy
Page 17: Keith Erskine/Alamy
Page 18: REX
Page 19: Sipa Press/REX
page 20: TopHat24/7 Productions, Inc.
Page 21: John T. Wong/Photolibrary/Getty Images
Page 22: Sang Tan/AP/Press Association Images
Page 23: John Eveson/FLPA/REX
Page 24: Nathan Benn/Alamy
Page 25: AFP/Stringer/Getty Images
Page 26: North Wind Picture Archives/Alamy
Page 27: Harald Slauschek/ASAblanca/Getty Images
Page 28: The Canadian Press/Press Association Images
Page 29: Andrew Woodley/Alamy
Page 30: Peter Casolino/Alamy

Attempts to contact all copyright holders have been made.
If any omitted would care to contact Badger Learning, we will be happy to make appropriate arrangements.

HIDDEN TREASURE

Contents

1. Amazing Finds

Treasure hunters search for treasure in the ground and under the sea. In particular, they search for lost or hidden riches, such as gold, silver and jewels.

A safe place

Before there were banks, people often buried
their money and other precious belongings in the
ground, or other secret places, to keep them safe.

The Staffordshire Hoard

In 2009, the biggest collection of Anglo-Saxon gold and
silver objects in the world was found in a farmer's field
in England, by a treasure hunter using a metal detector.

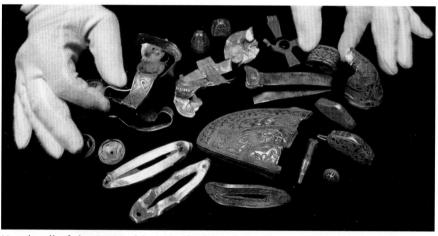

Nearly all of the 3,500 objects in the hoard are from military items, such as
swords and helmets.

WOW! facts

The finder of the Staffordshire
Hoard was given a reward of *over
£3 million* to share with the farmer
on whose land it was found.

Ancient burials

In ancient times, rich and important people were often buried with their most valuable belongings.

Sutton Hoo

In the grounds of Sutton Hoo House, in England, there are 18 large grassy mounds. They have been there for over a thousand years. For a long time, no one knew what they were.

Then, in 1939, the owner of Sutton Hoo asked an archaeologist to dig into the mounds to find out what they were.

The archaeologist discovered that they were part of an ancient burial site.

The largest mound is thought to be the grave of an Anglo-Saxon king buried in a treasure-filled ship.

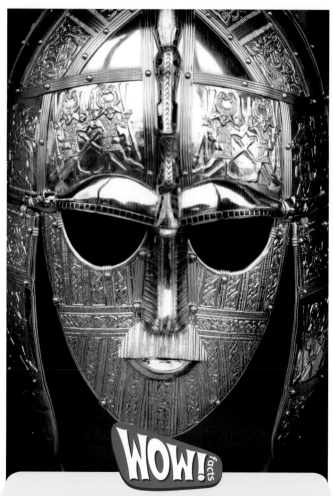

WOW! facts

Though the king's priceless belongings were found, his body was not. Even his bones had completely decayed!

Treasure is sometimes found in ships that have been wrecked in a storm.

Our Lady of Atocha

In 1622, a ship was sailing to Spain when it was hit by a hurricane.

Smashed to pieces on a coral reef, the ship, its cargo of silver, gold and emeralds, and almost all of its crew disappeared beneath the waves.

A new search

Almost 350 years later, an American treasure hunter, called Mel Fisher, began searching for the ship.

It took Mel and his team *16 years* but they finally found it in 1985!

There was so much treasure on board *Our Lady of Atocha*, it took two months to record and load it all!

It is thought the treasure Mel found in the ship is worth over 450 *million* dollars!

Lost at sea

Ships also sometimes sink because they are attacked or because of human error.

The Nanking Cargo

In 1751, a ship carrying porcelain and gold left China on its way to Holland.

The weather was fine and the seas were good but the ship never arrived. A mistake by the ship's crew caused the ship to crash into a reef.

WOW! facts

The Nanking Cargo did not smash when the ship hit the reef because it had been packed into crates of tea!

An amazing find

The ship then lay hidden under metres of silt for over 260 years until it was found by Captain Michael Hatcher.

Captain Hatcher managed to rescue 150,000 pieces of porcelain and 125 gold bars from the ship. They were sold for *over 20 million dollars*!

2. TREASURE HUNTERS

For a few people, treasure hunting is their job. It is how they make their living.

Full time treasure hunters, like Mel Fisher and Captain Michael Hatcher, are usually qualified divers, too, who search for lost and stolen treasure in shipwrecks.

Dr E Lee Spence

Underwater archaeologist and treasure hunter,
Dr E Lee Spence, has been interested in shipwrecks
and treasure hunting since he was a child.
He qualified as a diver when he was just 15
and has discovered hundreds of shipwrecks
in his career.

By the age of 12, Dr Spence
had already discovered five
shipwrecks!

Being a treasure hunter can
be dangerous work. Dr Spence
has been attacked by sharks, become
lost inside a wreck – *and* run out of air!

Digging up the past

Archaeologists study history by digging up objects from the past. They find all kinds of interesting objects hidden underground or in wrecked ships. The objects they find are often rare and valuable, too.

Howard Carter

Howard Carter was an English archaeologist. He was working in Egypt nearly 100 years ago when he uncovered some steps leading underground. The steps led down to a sealed door. Behind the door was the tomb of an Egyptian boy-king called Tutankhamen. The tomb was packed with treasures!

Like many of the objects in Tutankhamen's tomb, the king's death mask was made of gold.

There was so much treasure in Tutankhamen's tomb, it took Carter ten years to carefully remove it all!

Metal detectors

Most treasure hunters are amateurs. Hunting for treasure is their hobby. They often use a metal detector to help them find treasure. The detector beeps when it is near anything made of metal.

Wearing headphones helps the treasure hunter hear the beeps more clearly.

The Harrogate Hoard

In 2007, a father and son in the UK were metal detecting when they discovered one of the biggest hoards of Viking silver ever found. It was worth over £1 million!

Golden Nugget

In 1980, Australian Kevin Hillier uncovered the largest nugget of gold ever found with a metal detector. It weighed over 27kg!

Some of the biggest finds of silver and gold in the world have been found with a metal detector.

Down to luck

Some *very lucky* people also stumble across treasure – by accident!

Lost and found

In 1992, a UK farmer asked a friend who had a metal detector if he could find a hammer he had lost in a field. His friend found the hammer *and* over £1.75 million worth of Roman gold and silver!

A lucky fall

About a hundred years ago, some boys were playing by a river in Russia. Suddenly, one of the boys fell through the sand. He had fallen into an old grave full of treasure!

WOW! facts

In 1940, in France, four teenagers were searching for their dog when they discovered some of the most amazing cave paintings in the world.

3. HOW TO FIND TREASURE

Finding sunken treasure is not easy. But there are some places where you are more likely to find it than others.

Some of the most likely places to find sunken treasure are in the seas around Mexico, Florida and the Caribbean islands.

There are also many wrecks in the Indian Ocean and the Mediterranean Sea.

Locating a wreck

To find a wreck, treasure hunters must first spend a long time studying old papers and maps to find out what cargo a ship was carrying and where it sank.

WOW! facts

Old wooden ships are especially difficult to find as the wood often rots away!

Finding treasure underground

It is especially difficult to find treasure that is hidden underground. Much of this kind of treasure is found accidentally when a piece of land is ploughed or is being cleared for building work.

These are part of a hoard of more than 400 pieces of jewellery that was found by builders in London in 1912.

Locating treasure

Treasure hunters can improve their chances of finding treasure by using a metal detector and by looking in an area where treasure has already been found.

But all treasure hunters must remember to get permission from the landowner *before* they start searching!

WOW! facts

Almost 90 per cent of treasure found in the UK is found by amateurs with metal detectors!

Making a discovery

If someone finds a treasure hoard, there are two things they should do.

1. They should **stop digging** and call in an expert to help. (An archaeologist will know the safest way to remove the treasure.)
2. They should **report their find** to the landowner and the local authorities.

Finders keepers

In some countries, finders can keep any treasure they find on their own land. But if the treasure is found on someone else's land, a court will decide who keeps it.

Rich rewards

In other countries, finders are *not* always allowed to keep the treasure. But they will often be offered a reward for it, which they must share with the landowner.

Not everyone wants a reward.
Some people donate their treasure
to a museum, without payment.

4. LOST TREASURE

Many valuable treasures have been missing for hundreds of years. Lots of people believe they are still hidden, just waiting to be found!

Missing in the mud

In England, in 1216, soldiers were transporting King John's crown jewels by cart. As they took a short cut across a river, they were cut off by the tide. The soldiers drowned and the treasure carts sank under the mud. To this day, they have never been found.

Pirate Island

In 1820, Captain William Thomson was asked to sail a ship loaded with treasure to Mexico. But the captain turned pirate and stole the treasure! He hid the treasure on Coco Island. But it has never been found.

350 tons of pirate gold is also thought to be buried somewhere on the island!

The Oak Island Money Pit

In 1795, some boys found a mysterious pit on a Canadian island, in an area visited by pirates. The boys started digging, looking for pirate's gold. But they found nothing of value.

Then, ten years later, a stone was dug up in the pit. The message on it said, in code: "Forty feet down, two million pounds are buried." People haven't stopped looking for the treasure since!

Can you spot the entrance to the money pit?

Why do you think it is fenced off?

Flower of the Sea

In 1511, a ship called *Flower of the Sea* was sailing to Portugal when it was caught in a violent storm. The ship broke in two and the vast treasure it was carrying was lost beneath the waves.

The cargo on board *Flower of the Sea* is thought to be the richest treasure still waiting to be found!

Treasure for everyone!

Geocaching

Geocaching is a kind of global treasure hunt that anyone can take part in. It is treasure hunting, just for fun and it's free!

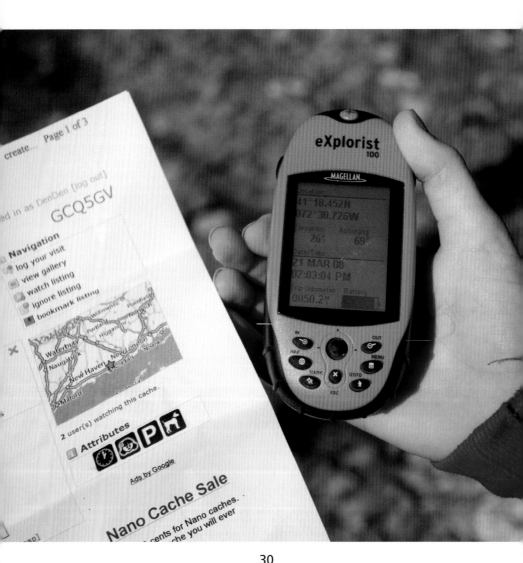

Geocachers hide boxes and other geocachers try to find them. The position of the hidden box is put online. Treasure hunters then try to find the box using GPS. Some geocaches are more difficult to find than others.

Whoops!
In 2011, a man was seen hiding a box under a rubbish bin in a street. Someone thought the man was planting a bomb and called the police. But it was just a geocacher hiding a box for other people to find!

There are over two million geocaches and six million geocachers worldwide! (You can learn more about geocaching at www.geocaching.com)

INDEX